IN GOD'S GRACE

Daily Meditations and Prayers
For the Season of Lent

In God's Grace

Daily Meditations and Prayers
For the Season of Lent

David H. Lester

Order this book online at www.trafford.com
or email orders@trafford.com

Most Trafford titles are also available at major online book retailers.

All funds from the sale of this book will be used for charitable purposes.

All Scripture references are from The New Oxford Annotated Bible with the
Apocrypha (Expanded Edition) Revised Standard Version, Copyright 1977,
New York, Oxford University Press 1977.

Printed in the United States of America.

ISBN: 978-1-4269-9252-0 (sc)
ISBN: 978-1-4269-9253-7 (e)

Library of Congress Control Number: 2011914534

Trafford rev. 08/18/2011

 www.trafford.com

North America & international
toll-free: 1 888 232 4444 (USA & Canada)
phone: 250 383 6864 ♦ fax: 812 355 4082

Dedication

To the

Glory of God

And

To my wife

Joyce Elaine Lester

Contents

Preface

This writing in its entirety comes straight from the heart. It finds its origin in a request made to me by the Rev. Carl B. Schreiber, Jr., Senior Pastor of East Orrington Congregational Church in Orrington, Maine. Pastor Carl asked if I would be willing to write a daily devotion for the season of Lent. I was pleased to be asked and set about the task of searching my own heart in preparation.

As a Christian and certainly as an ordained minister the season of Lent is very important to me. However, I must confess that in the writing of the daily devotions you will be reading, the season of Lent took on a whole new meaning and depth for me as an individual soul. I explored and prayed more deeply than ever before concerning my own sin, my relationship with God, Jesus Christ, and the Holy Spirit, as well as the life I am living in response to God's immeasurable love for me. I took to heart the core Lenten concept of self-evaluation in light of the saving acts of God through Jesus Christ.

In recent days I was moved by God to share these meditations with as many people as possible. I decided to put them into print allowing for the opportunity to have them readily available to anyone who chooses to use them in devotion. In rereading the material it also became clear to me that most of the meditations can be used outside the season of Lent. Self-examination before God is not confined to the Lenten season alone. I leave it up to you, the reader, whether you use the material strictly for the season of Lent, or whether you refer to it from time to time as a daily devotion.

I encourage you to take the time to read all of the readings for each day and to sincerely meditate upon the guidance given in the meditations. The mediations are intended only as a starting point. From there you are encouraged to reflect more specifically about your personal life and your relationship with the Triune God. Likewise I encourage you to expand the prayers to be more specific about you and your response to God's love. I pray that as you work your way through these readings you will come to know the full joy and reality, as did I, of living "In God's Grace".

David H. Lester

FIRST WEEK OF LENT

Ash Wednesday

Ash Wednesday begins the season of Lent which covers the 46 days (40 not counting Sundays) before Easter. Ashes formed by the burning of palms from the previous year's Palm Sunday are mixed with a small amount of oil to create a paste. The officiating minister places ashes in the shape of a cross on the foreheads of those who come forth as a sign of repentance. Lent is a time during which Christians go through a period of repentance and self-examination.

Scripture Readings:

Psalter: Psalm 32

Old Testament: Jonah 3:1-4:11

Epistle: Hebrews 12:1-14

Gospel: Luke 18:9-14

Meditation: True confession and repentance comes from deep within the soul. Repentance is far more than words passing through our lips. It is a recognition of, and deep regret for, our sins of commission and our sins of omission. Further, repentance is a true commitment to self and to God that we will stop, turn around, and move in the opposite direction of our transgressions. As we take the Lenten journey, God calls each of us to begin that journey, standing fully exposed before God, holding nothing back, and acknowledging the depth of our sin. No matter to what depths we may have fallen from grace, we are never so far away that God is not with us. "Whither shall I go from thy Spirit?" (Psalm 139:7a) God also calls us to stand before Christ our Saviour as we pour out our heart-felt thanksgiving that Jesus took our individual and collective sins upon himself.

Prayer:

Holy God of Eternal Forgiveness, I come in these quiet moments I have set aside to be with you. I come to confess the fullness of my sinful self. There are sins of long ago such as (lift to God your sins) and there are sins of recent days such as (lift to God your sins). It is hard, Lord, for me to speak these sins out loud. It is hard to even raise them once more in my own heart and mind. They weigh so heavy upon my heart and in these moments I humbly pray for your forgiveness – that forgiveness made possible through the saving acts of Jesus Christ. Bless me Holy God of Compassion, and encourage me to take full advantage of this Lenten Season. Help me to fully examine myself. Help me to face fully my fears and those obstacles which I have allowed to stand between me and Thee. Help me use this time not only to speak, but to listen quietly as I strive to discern your will for me. I make this prayer in the name of Jesus Christ, your Son, whom I acknowledge and accept anew this day as my Lord and my Savior. Amen.

*****

Thursday of Week One

Scripture Readings:

Psalter: Psalm 37:1-18

Old Testament: Deuteronomy 7:6-11

Epistle: Titus 1:1-16

Gospel: John 1:29-34

Meditation: "Trust in the Lord, and do good; so you will dwell in the land, and enjoy security. Take delight in the Lord, and he will give you the desires of your heart" (Psalm 37:3-4). Today is a day to think and to pray about trust. We need to trust that the Word of God that has come to us through Scripture, discernment, and other people in our life is a Word that will be fulfilled. We need to recall God's own words through the prophet Isaiah, "My Word that goes forth from my mouth; it shall not return to me empty, but it shall accomplish that which I purpose, and prosper in the thing for which I sent it." (Isaiah 55:11) To find true happiness we need to begin by more fully trusting God. God is a God of Covenant and has never broken a covenant made with all humanity or with a single person. However, there is more trust than our trusting God. We need to discern if God can trust us. While we are trusting God to fulfill His promises to us as a people and as an individual, are we equally as eager for God to be able to trust us? Can God trust us to keep the promises, the covenants, we make?

Prayer:

Precious Lord, in whom I put my utmost trust, help me daily to strengthen that trust. Likewise help me daily to give you cause to more easily trust the promises and covenants I make, not only with you, but with self and with other people. Help me to better understand that by fully trusting in you, there is nothing in life that I cannot move through. Forgive those times when I actually doubt you have my best interest at heart. It is selfish of me and falls short of the trust and praise you so richly deserve. Forgive me when I have blamed you for the condition of my life. Forgive me when it seems to me you have let me down. Truly these are utterings of a weak, frightened, and exhausted heart. Lord, it is easy to trust you when things in my life are going well. Help me to trust you when it seems, at least for the moment, that my life is falling apart around me. Remind me that there are times you calm the storm that is raging about me, and there are other times when you calm me in the midst of the storm, allowing the storm to rage on. As I move through this Lenten Season, help me to find a new level of trust in the very origin of my being. Amen

*****

Friday of Week One

Scripture Readings:

Psalter: Psalm 31

Old Testament: Deuteronomy 7:12-16

Epistle: Titus 2:1-15

Gospel: John 1:35-42

Meditation: "We have found the Messiah" (John 1:41b)! We can only imagine the excitement that ran through the entire being of Andrew as he told his brother, Simon Peter, that he found the Messiah. Often when we think of people being found we say they have found each other. If two boys wander away from each other while playing in the woods, when they finally find one another we do not say that one boy found the other; rather we say the two boys found each other. God the Father, Son and Holy Spirit has always known where you are. No matter how lost you have become, no matter how far into the darkness you have ventured, God has always been present. It is you who needs to find God. It is you who God guides in the right direction that one day, in a very clarifying moment, you can say from the very depths of your soul, "I have found the Messiah!" As you examine your life during this season of Lent, give thought today to the faith that Jesus, the Messiah, has already found you. When you have found the Messiah, then it can be said that you have found one another.

Prayer: Holy God who is always nearer to me than my very next breath, I praise you in these moments of meditation, acknowledging that you are ever with me, in the good times and in the rough times. I confess, Lord, that I have sometimes strayed from the path upon which you lead me. I confess that when I follow my own path I am lost. Yet, Lord, you have always kept me within reach. You have always watched over me. And when I find you, I see your hand of salvation already stretched out toward me. You welcome me back into your presence. Help me, Blessed Jesus, to ever keep close to you. Help me to live the life you have given me in such a way that those around me will proclaim, "Truly this person has found the Messiah!" Amen

*****

Saturday of Week One

Scripture Readings:

Psalter: Psalm 42

Old Testament: Deuteronomy 7:17-26

Epistle: Titus 3:1-15

Gospel: John 1:43-51

Meditation: "[God] saved us, not because of deeds done by us in righteousness, but in virtue of His own mercy" (Titus 3:5). Writing to Titus, the Apostle Paul lifts up a portion of the very foundation of his own faith and theology. Paul's theological statement is one which holds that salvation comes, not from anything we have done or can do; rather salvation comes only from the grace and mercy of God. However, we cannot sit back and do nothing. We are called to live our life in response to God's unfettered gift of salvation. Most of us have fallen short of this call. Today is a day to praise God and thank God for the very gift of salvation. It is a day to confess your own sins, to truly regret having sinned before God, and to seek God's assistance as you strive in this very moment to live that life God intended for you.

Prayer: Merciful God, as I sit in the quietness of the moment, I reflect upon and acknowledge my sins. Before I was ever born you knew me and you called me by name. You breathed your Spirit into me that others may see and experience God wherever I go. There are times I have tarnished this honor and have truly fallen short of your expectations for me. Yet, in your mercy you still forgive me. You have given me a clean slate, a fresh start. It is as though my sin never occurred. Blessed Lord, you know my weakness. You know it more than anyone else including me. My very soul which has been made heavy by my sin is now light and free because of your forgiveness. When I recognize the depth of your love for me, it brings tears of joy to my eyes and a song of thanksgiving to my soul. By your love, by your grace, by your mercy you have saved me; and I give you all honor and praise. Amen

Sunday of Week One

Scripture Readings:

Psalter: Psalm 103

Old Testament: Deuteronomy 8:1-10

Epistle: 1 Corinthians 1:17-31

Gospel: Matthew 9:14-17

Meditation: Moses tells the people of Israel, "You shall remember all the ways which the Lord your God has led you these forty years in the wilderness" (Deut. 8:2). The Israelite's journey through the wilderness is often referred to as a wandering. They were truly a people who felt they had no place to call home. The Israelite's were tempted while in the wilderness and truly they fell dramatically from grace. They turned their attention to idols, tangible objects of worship, and turned away from God. For the most part this tragic event took place because the Israelite's did not like God's time schedule. They believed God led them into the desert to die, when actually God led them there to save them. How many times have we found ourselves in a wilderness place? How many times have we felt that God has led us astray? Even though we may not have allowed these words to pass our lips, we must confess there have been times when such was the feelings of our heart. Today, ponder upon those times in your life when you were in a wilderness place; a time when you felt your world was falling in around you. Ponder the reality of the presence of God in that time and in those moments. Ponder the sense of relief you felt when you suddenly discovered you were no longer in the wilderness; that God had indeed been with you and led you to a new place.

Prayer: God of all who find themselves wandering in desert places, I remember those times when I was in such a wilderness I thought I would never find my way out. The truth is, God, I never did find my own way out. The truth is that you embraced me; you sheltered me; you gave me just the amount of energy, encouragement, and confidence I needed. Then it was truly you, Lord, who led me out of the wilderness and welcomed me into the Promised Land, a land where I knew beyond any doubt I was in the presence of the Most High. Help me to remember always the grace and mercy with which you have changed my life. Grant that I will always, not simply be grateful, but live a life in response to your love. Help me to put complete faith in you such that I do not draw weary when it seems I have been in the desert much too long. Remind me over and over that you are with me and you will make the journey with me because you are my God, and I am one of your people. Amen

*****

SECOND WEEK OF LENT

Monday of Week Two

Scripture Readings:

Psalter: Psalm 41

Old Testament: Deuteronomy 8:11-18

Epistle: Hebrews 2:11-18

Gospel: John 2:1-12

Meditation: "This, the first of his signs, Jesus did at Cana in Galilee, and manifested his glory; and his disciples believed in him" (John 2:11). Jesus' act of turning water into wine was evidence enough for his disciples to believe he was truly the Messiah sent from God. It is important to note that Jesus is not a magician. He does not turn water into wine for the sake of entertainment. In fact, Jesus could have just as easily just said what a shame it was to be out of wine at such a festive time. However, what Jesus did do was to take advantage of a situation. He needed an earthly way to help those around him understand the heavenly power. When we look at our own lives we are very aware there have been times when we were totally at a loss. Either we did not know how to handle a certain situation or we were for some reason feeling distant from God, or perhaps feeling distant for Christ's Church. It was then that God through Jesus Christ brought a miracle into our life. It was then than God took what was insufficient, broken, or tarnished, and either restored it to its former condition or in some cases turned it into something even better. We can all point to times in our life when we were so down we thought surely we would never experience being up again. Yet, God, in His mercy brings a miracle to our life. As we witness the miracle, not only are we grateful, but our faith and our confidence in God is strengthened because we have been the beneficiary of God's grace.

Prayer: Precious Lord, I come to you with a grateful heart this day asking that you will open my eyes to all the moments, large and small, when you have brought a miracle into my life and/or into the lives of those I love. Forgive me, Lord, for those times when my faith falters; those times when I want to believe you will come through for me and yet I am afraid you might not. Forgive me for doubting your ability. Forgive me for doubting that you care enough for me to never leave me alone to fend for myself. Forgive me for not telling everyone I meet of the wondrous acts of God in my life. Thank you, God, for bringing such miracles into my life that I can truly believe. Thank you, Lord, for helping me to believe. Forgive me, Lord, for my disbelief. Amen.

*****

Tuesday of Week Two

Scripture Readings:

Psalter: Psalm 48

Old Testament: Deuteronomy 9:4-12

Epistle: Hebrews 3:1-11

Gospel: John 2:13-22

Meditation: Jesus said to the money changers, "You shall not make my Father's house a house of trade." (John 2:16). These words were spoken by Jesus because he believed the temple was being defiled as it was being used for a purpose for which it was not intended. In his first letter to the Church at Corinth, the Apostle Paul asked, "Do you not know that your body is a temple of the Holy Spirit within you, which you have from God?" (1 Cor. 6:19a). The question we should ponder is this: "Are we using our life for a purpose other than that which God intends?" Certainly we must agree in the short term that we all are guilty in certain places and certain moments in our life. Paul goes on to say, "You are not your own; you were bought for a price. So glorify God in your body." (1 Cor. 6:19b-20). Take time today to reflect upon your life. Reflect upon those times when you used your life for a purpose other than that which God intends. Reflect upon those times your actions indicated you had actually said, "No" to God.

Prayer: God of Love, it brings great pain to the core of my soul as I confess to you that I have at times used my life for something other than what you intend.   I am further disheartened when I consider that such actions are evidence that I chose to say "no" to you in a given moment. Lord, I can only ask for your mercy.   I can only ask for your forgiveness.   I acknowledge that I am not worthy of such love in and of myself.   However, you, O God, have made me worthy through your Son Jesus Christ.   As such you have chosen to forgive me for this and all my sins.   You have chosen to set me again on that path that leads to righteousness.   For this and all your countless blessings I give you my praise and my gratitude. Amen

*****

Wednesday of Week Two

Scripture Readings:

Psalter: Psalm 119:49-72

Old Testament: Deuteronomy 9:13-21

Epistle: Hebrews 3:12-19

Gospel: John 2:23-3:15

Meditation: Moses told the people of Israel what God had said concerning them: "I have seen this people, and behold, it is a stubborn people" (Deut. 9:13a). There is a certain level when we humans will freely crack a joke about God calling the Israelites stubborn. We have been known to make merriment out of people of long ago as well as people of today using God's own words as fodder for our own enjoyment. God's words were not meant just for the Hebrew people of so many years ago. God's words are meant for you and me today. How often has God found himself saying of any of us, "I have seen this person, and behold he/she is a stubborn person?" Sometimes we are stubborn because even though we are fully certain God is pulling us in a particular direction; we are digging our heels in and trying with all our might to flee in the opposite direction as a course for our life. Perhaps God has seen some of us as stubborn when we fail or even decline to see the good that we do in this community and in the world at large. Perhaps we are stubborn when we are hesitant to make change in our life. Perhaps we are stubborn when we do not trust God enough to bring new life to our being. Perhaps we are sometimes so stubborn we forget that we are made in the very image of God and we are called to live as such. Today is a good day to reflect upon these things. Today is a good day to take measure of our own stubbornness before God.

Prayer: Holy God of Stubborn People, I thank you in these moments for continuing to be the God of this stubborn person – me. I thank you for not giving up on me. I thank you for granting me the courage to examine my life in light of who it is you call me to be. I thank you for guiding me in such a way that in the midst of your forgiveness I can truly find my way back to being the person you know I can be. Like so many things in life, Lord, I cannot do this on my own. I need and I ask for your help. I confess my stubbornness. I confess even my reluctance to change who I am. I confess that all too often I am more interested in getting you to accept who I am than in getting myself to be more like the person you call me to be. Bless me this day, dear Lord. Grant me the peace of knowing you continue to be God. Amen.

*****

Thursday of Week Two

Scripture Readings:

Psalter: Psalm 19

Old Testament: Deuteronomy 9:23-10:5

Epistle: Hebrews 4:1-10

Gospel: John 3:16-21

Meditation: "For good news came to us just as to them; but the message which they heard did not benefit them, because it did not meet with faith in the hearers" (Hebrews 4:2). The problem the author of Hebrews is bringing out in 4:2 is more common today than most people would care to believe or even acknowledge. God's Word comes to us from many sources. God's Word comes to us as God places it upon our hearts; it comes through sermons, through reading scripture, through the ministry of fellowship, through doing with and for others, through the actions of children and adults alike, through the rich and the poor, through the marginalized, and even through our enemies just to name a few. How many times have we heard the Word of God and it fell on deaf ears or a hardened heart? How many times have we heard the Word of God and failed to have faith in that Word because we did not like the source? Today is the day to confess before God that you have at times allowed His Word to fall on deaf ears. It is time to confess that we have tuned out the message just because we did not care for the messenger.

Prayer: God of all Creation who called the world into being by uttering the Word, I praise your mighty name this day. I bow before you, Lord, acknowledging that I have at times turned a deaf ear to your Word, not so much because I did not like the Word, but more because the Word came from one of my enemies, or from someone I thought less of. Forgive me, God, as you remind me that your Word will never return unto you void. Forgive me when I have chosen to ignore your Word simply because I did not trust the message given the person through whom it came. Remind me, Lord, that you use all people to your glory. Amen.

*****

Friday of Week Two

Scripture Readings:

Psalter: Psalm 51

Old Testament: Deuteronomy 10:12-22

Epistle: Hebrews 4:1-16

Gospel: John 3:22-36

Meditation: God is living and active in our lives, "discerning the thoughts and intentions of the heart." (Hebrews 4:12b). The author of Hebrews is very clear that God takes no passive role in our lives. On the contrary, God is living and very active in our lives. One of the very active things God does in our life is to discern the thoughts and intentions of the heart. This is extremely important for us to comprehend. While it may be true that our mouth says one thing, it is also often true that our heart says quite another thing. God looks very carefully at the intentions that are found in our heart. Sometimes it is not our intention to hurt another human being and yet we do. Sometimes it is not our intention to ignore the presence of God in our life. However, there are those times, we must admit, that we are so out of touch with God it is as though He is a stranger. God looks more to our intentions than He looks at our successes and failures. God wants to know if we have tried. God wants to know if we have used every ounce of our knowledge and have called upon the assistance of every person whose name we can think of. Today is the day for you to discern the true thoughts and intentions of your own heart. Today is the day to make sure the intentions of your heart are in sync with the expectations of God.

Prayer: Holy God of Discernment, bless me this day as I come before you in these moments to confess that my intentions have not always been the best they could be. I confess that sometimes I take the easier or the preferred road. Sometimes I take a different path simply because I want to. Forgive me, I pray. Restore to me that relationship with you that I once enjoyed. Restore to me the faith I need to put confidence in what you are doing for this world and even for my own little world. Thank you for discerning the thoughts and intentions of my heart. Grant me a stronger, more faithful heart. This and all prayers I ask in the name of Jesus Christ. Amen.

*****

Saturday of Week Two

Scripture Readings:

Psalter: Psalm 55

Old Testament: Deuteronomy 11:18-28

Epistle: Hebrews 5:1-10

Gospel: John 4:1-26

Meditation: "But I call upon God; and the Lord will save me" (Psalm 55:16). Psalm 55 is a Psalm of David in which he is asking God for deliverance from his new found enemy. The primary enemy at this time is one who was once David's friend. Perhaps that has happened to you at some point. Perhaps you and another person were real close friends for many years. Suddenly that person turns against you, uttering all manner of ill talk about you. But let's draw this closer home. Let's take a look at ourselves. Who among us has not at some time become our own worst enemy? The very core of salvation is God's grace to save each of us from ourselves. It is ourselves from whom we need protection because we are the ones who are often making bad choices. We are the ones who are often going against what we know to be the will of God. We pick from the tree of life that God tells us we should leave alone. We refuse to pick from the tree that God tells us will fulfill us. All too often we can be found eating from the "tree of thinking we know better than God". It is in those very times that we need to bow before God, seeking the forgiveness that only

He can provide, and seek His help in blazing a new path in life. Indeed, today is the day to call upon God, for surely He will save us.

Prayer: Holy God of salvation, I come to you with a humble heart. I come knowing full well I have all too often eaten from the wrong tree. I come knowing that for as much as I assail those who I see as my enemies, I am at times my own worst enemy. It is I, and I alone, who steers me away from you. It is I who has chosen to eat of the wrong tree. It is I who has thought I know better than God. While these words have not passed my lips, my actions and/or my inactions have at times proclaimed them loudly. It is for this, O Lord, that I come seeking forgiveness. Mend my soul, O God. Restore me to my rightful self. Guide me such that I become the person you knew I could be when you called me into being. "Give ear to my prayer, O God; and hide not thyself from my supplication! Attend to me, and answer me; I am overcome by my trouble". (Psalm 55:1-2). Amen

*****

Sunday of Week Two

Scripture Readings:

Psalter: Psalm 29

Old Testament: Jeremiah 1:1-10

Epistle: 1 Corinthians 3:11-23

Gospel: Matthew 13:1-9

Meditation: "Before I formed you in the womb I knew you, and before you were born I consecrated you; I appointed you a prophet to the nations" (Jeremiah 1:5). The Word of God spoken to Jeremiah is the same Word of God spoken to us. God knew each of us long before we were born. He called us by name and consecrated us to a particular role in the life of this planet we call earth. As we move through life trying to discern the will of God for us, we will find that God is always there, giving us clues. There are times we are guilty of pretending we do not know what God is calling us to do. There are times when we are certain that God must be mistaken and is really trying to call someone else. Today is that time when we need to offer to God our greatest joy and thanksgiving for calling us to be who were are even before we were actually born. Today is the day to acknowledge that we have each been consecrated to a specific role in this world. We have all too often taken on a different role, the role of sinner. This is why we need to bring our lives and our faults before God, seeking once again His grace and His mercy.

Prayer: O Holy God of Great Wisdom, I thank you that I am not left to my own devices. I thank you that even though I sometimes wish I was, I am not fully in charge of the scope and direction of my life. For as much as I call it my life, truly it is a life that belongs to you. Lord, forgive me for those times I have ignored your direction in favor of something that seemed more pleasant to me. Forgive me for the times I have pretended I do not know that I have been consecrated for a specific purpose in this world. Forgive me when I take on the role of sinner. It is a role I often play all too well. I thank you and praise your Holy Name for once again showering me with your mercy which comes in the form of forgiveness. Help me Lord to fully understand that to which you have called me. Encourage me to set it as a primary goal in my life; a goal toward which I can work a little each day. I ask this in Jesus' name. Amen

*****

THIRD WEEK OF LENT

Monday of Week Three

Scripture Readings:

Psalter: Psalm 56

Old Testament: Jeremiah 1:11-19

Epistle: Romans 1:1-5

Gospel: John 4:27-42

Meditation: "Come and see a man who told me everything I ever did. Can this be the Christ? (John 4:29). The woman at the well marveled that Jesus knew so much about her. She was so impressed that she asked if this could be the Christ. The question arises if we have looked into our own life and asked, "Can this be the Christ working within me?" When the woman went to draw water that day she did not expect to be approached by the Christ of God. Yet, that is exactly what happened. There are many times in our own lives when God in Christ Jesus comes suddenly to the forefront, taking us by surprise, and moving us in new directions. There are indeed those times when we get into the rhythm of our own daily life that we sometimes forget about the very existence of God, much less the very presence of God. Today is a good day to remind ourselves that God does truly exist; that He not only exists for the world and all creation, but He exists very real for each of us. Today is a good day to rekindle that personal relationship with Jesus Christ; that relationship you know will turn your life into something far beyond your fondest dreams.

Prayer: Holy God who often meets us in unimaginable places and at unexpected times, I come to you this day asking that you will help me to get closer to you. Help me Lord to develop or strengthen my personal relationship with Christ. Help me to take to heart the reality of Jesus taking my sins upon himself that I might not only live, but will have eternal life. I pray, God, that you will forgive me for those times I did recognize Jesus and yet turned to go in a different direction. Help me to truly know who it is who is offering me the living water. Forgive me when I take the reality and power of the living water for granted. I ask this in Jesus' name. Amen.

*****

Tuesday of Week Three

Scripture Readings:

Psalter: Psalm 62

Old Testament: Jeremiah 2:1-13

Epistle: Romans 1:16-25

Gospel: John 4:43-54

Meditation: In his letter to the Church at Rome the Apostle Paul said, "I am not ashamed of the gospel; it is the power of God for salvation to everyone who has faith." (Romans 11:16a). Paul's words are very important to Christians today. All too often Christians are indeed ashamed of the gospel. They are ashamed to be seen carrying a Bible in public unless surrounded by other Christians who are also carrying their Bibles. Too often Christians today claim to not be ashamed of the Gospel Message and yet so very few have actually read the text upon which they claim to base their life. In other words, there is the faith based on hearing Scripture read during worship and there is faith based on personally reading the Scripture, sitting with Scripture, allowing oneself to be convicted by Scripture. Given the opportunity to spend two hours reading the latest best seller or a new book written by one's favorite author, versus spending two hours reading Scripture, the average Christian would choose to read that which is not Scripture. Today is the day to ask yourself why you do not know Scripture as well as you know other books. Today is the day to ask yourself what authority you give to Scripture in your life. Today is the day to commit yourself to reading and studying the infallible Word of God found in the fallible word of man. Today is the day to determine what influence Scripture has in your life.

Prayer: Holy God of every human soul, I come before you in these moments aware that I have certainly not read or studied Scripture as I should. I know that contained within Scripture is your Word for me and all humanity. I pray that you will help me to arrange my life and my priorities such that I will truly give balance to reading Scripture. I am aware I will not fully understand everything I read. However, I also know that I need to commit to being more familiar with the Word of God by my own efforts, not just what is read to me by others. Bless me, Lord, this day, and help me to keep my promise and commitment to you and to myself. I ask this in Jesus' Holy Name. Amen

*****

Wednesday of Week Three

Scripture Readings:

Psalter: Psalm 119:73-96

Old Testament: Jeremiah 3:6-18

Epistle: Romans 1:28-2:11

Gospel: John 5:1-18

Meditation: In John's account of the gospel Jesus asks a lame man, "Do you want to be healed" (John 5:6b)? What an absolutely powerful question this is! Do you want to be healed? Not even knowing who Jesus was at the time, the lame man put his faith in God, not in the man speaking with him. So when Jesus told the lame man to pick up his pallet and walk, he did so without hesitation. It was truly the proverbial faith as small as a mustard seed. It was the faith that could move mountains and throw them into the sea. During this time of Lent when you are going through a period of self-evaluation, you are encouraged to answer the question, "Do you want to be healed?" What is your great ailment in life? What is it that you need healing from? There are many who will rush to the physical. Or they will rush to the mental and emotional. You are encouraged to seek healing in your spiritual relationship with God. Do you want to be healed badly enough to follow the wisdom of God? Do you have such faith that you would act without hesitation?

Prayer: God of all healing power, I come to you this day handing over to you all that burdens my soul. I especially give over to you the need for healing our relationship. I know, Lord, that you have kept your side of the covenant. It is me, Lord, who has broken the covenant. It is me who has let the relationship suffer. It is me whose life would greatly improve if only I would strengthen my ties with you. I ask you in Jesus' name to forgive my sins, and I ask that you will heal not only my physical needs, but also that you will heal and strengthen our relationship. Guide me, Lord, as I endeavor to embark on a new spiritual journey. Grant me the ability and indeed the desire to hold up my side of the covenant. I ask this in Jesus' Holy Name. Amen.

*****

Thursday of Week Three

Scripture Readings:

Psalter: Psalm 71

Old Testament: Jeremiah 4:9-10, 19-28

Epistle: Romans 2:12-24

Gospel: John 5:19-29

Meditation: Jesus said, "Truly, truly, I say to you, he who hears my word and believes him who sent me, has eternal life" (John 5:24a). As we take a deeper look at ourselves during Lent we are called to discern the true depth of our faith. As Christians we are asked by Jesus, "Do you believe the one who sent me?" In other words, "Do you believe God?" We are called to discern if we believe, for example, that "God sent His Son into the world not to condemn the world, but that the world through Him might be saved." (John 3:17). Do we believe on faith alone the Word and promises of the One who said, "I will walk among you and be your God, and you shall be my people." (Leviticus 26:12). Today you are encouraged to sit in prayer with God. Talk with God about the very nature of your faith. Place your faith in the light of Christ that it might be seen as it truly is.

Prayer: Gracious God of Faith and Discernment, I come to you this day to sit quietly with you as together we discern the true depth of my faith. Forgive me, Lord, where and when I have stumbled. Forgive me when I have failed to understand. Lift me to heights I have never known as my faith in you grows stronger with each passing day. Lord, grant that my faith when tested can be pronounced sound. Bless me, Lord, as you and I grow closer together in the I-Thou relationship. Help me to truly believe in you above all else. I ask this in the name of the one whom you sent to teach us all, Jesus Christ, my Lord and my Savior. Amen

*****

Friday of Week Three

Scripture Readings:

Psalter: Psalm 73

Old Testament: Jeremiah 5:1-9

Epistle: Romans 2:25-3:18

Gospel: John 5:30-47

Meditation: Jesus in talking about His relationship with God says, "I seek not my own will but that of the one who sent me" (John 5:30b). Today you are encouraged to look deeply into your own life to discern how closely you follow the example set so clearly by Jesus. If we are going to call ourselves Christians, we need to be sure that we actually follow the life example and the teachings of Jesus Christ. This is a time for brutal honesty. In your daily life do you tend to truly seek the will of God as exemplified by Jesus, or do you really seek your own will with the hope and prayer that it will meet with God's approval?

Prayer: Blessed Lord, it is difficult to admit that I often seek my own will over yours. It is difficult to admit that I sometimes just hope that you will approve of what it is that I want to do, or what it is that I want to see happen. Lord, I know that I cannot truly be happy unless I am in the protection of your will for me, not only in this life, but in that life that is yet to come. Help me, Lord, to cry out with Jesus in all things, "nevertheless, not my will by thy will be done"! I boldly ask this is Jesus' Name. Amen

*****

Saturday of Week Three

Scripture Readings:

Psalter: Psalm 75

Old Testament: Jeremiah 5:20-31

Epistle: Romans 3:19-31

Gospel: John 7:1-13

Meditation: Talking to His brothers, James, Joseph, Simon and Judas, Jesus said, "My time has not yet come, but your time is always here" (John 7:6). Jesus said this because His brothers were trying to get Jesus to publicly proclaim He is the Son of God at the Jewish Feast of the Tabernacles to be held in Judea. Jesus told His brothers that while it was not yet time (His time) to reveal His relationship to God, their time has come to reveal their relationship to God and to Jesus as His disciples. As Jesus said to His brothers, He also says to you, "Your time is always here." It is always your time to acknowledge God as your Heavenly Father. It is always your time to acknowledge Jesus Christ as your Lord and Savior. It is always time to live your life publically as a child of God and a disciple of Jesus Christ such that there will be no mistake by others. The world will know your relationship with the Holy Trinity by the way you live. As you examine your true self during Lent, ask yourself, "Do I live publically as a child of God and a disciple of Jesus Christ?"

Prayer: Heavenly Father who knows the right time for all that is and shall be, I pray that you will help me to fully understand that now, in this moment, is my time to live as a child of God and a disciple of Jesus Christ. Help me to know that my time for such true living is always. Holy God, I confess that I have not always lived up to your expectations. I confess that I have not in every circumstance lived in response to your love. I pray that in your tender mercy you will forgive me for this and all my sins. Truly it is against you, and only you, that I have sinned. Grant me the desire, the courage, and the tenacity to strive ever faithfully to proclaim in the here and now – "I am a child of God! I am a Christian – a disciple of Jesus Christ." Oh God, my God, all praise and glory to your Name. Amen

*****

Sunday of Week Three

Scripture Readings:

Psalter: Psalm 34

Old Testament: Jeremiah 6:9-15

Epistle: 1 Corinthians 6:12-20

Gospel: Matthew 8:28-34

Meditation: Mark tells of the time Jesus removed demons from a tortured man. While all three of the synoptic gospels tell this same story, Matthew goes an additional step saying, Jesus said to the man from whom He had removed the unclean spirit, "Go..tell...how much the Lord has done for you, and how He has had mercy on you" (Mark 5:19). As you meditate upon this portion of Scripture, give prayerful thought to all the many specific times you are very much aware of what God has done for you, and all the many times you are very much aware that God has shown you mercy. When you are true to yourself and with God you will discover there are countless things God has done for you, and equally a countless number of times when God has shown you mercy. As you think of these things, also reflect upon the fact there are also numerous things God has done for you, and numerous times God has shown you mercy when you were not even aware. How do you live your life in response to God's mercy? How do you respond to God's positive activity in your life? Do you praise God with your whole being? Do you acknowledge that God's grace and mercy are true gifts simply because God loves you? Meditate this day upon God's presence and mercy in your life.

Prayer: God of all Mercy, I stand before you in the quiet of these moments acknowledging my personal need for your presence in my life and for the never-ending mercy you heap upon me. I can name the following as very specific times when I know you were active in my life, and the following times when I know you bestowed your loving mercy upon me......(repeat those times and situations to God). While I know you are already aware of all these times, Lord, it is helpful for me to say them to you, lifting up my own awareness of your never-ending love. Lord, in the scheme of things I know that in and of myself I am not worthy of your love, your grace, or your forgiveness. Yet, I am also fully aware that because it pleases you to do so, you do in fact love me far beyond my human ability to comprehend. I accept your love, Lord, and I pray with all my heart that you will help me live my life, the life you give me on a daily basis, in response to your love and presence in my life. I make this prayer in Jesus' Holy Name. Amen.

*****

FOURTH WEEK OF LENT

Monday of Week Four

Scripture Readings:

Psalter: Psalm 80

Old Testament: Jeremiah 7:1-15

Epistle: Romans 4:1-12

Gospel: John 7:14-36

Meditation: The Psalmist lifts his voice to the heavens and cries "Restore us, O God; let thy face shine, that we may be saved" (Psalm 80:3)! The totality of Psalm 80 is a prayer to God for deliverance from enemies. When you think of needing God's help to deliver you from the aggressive actions of an enemy, it is well to remember that often times that very enemy is you. It is truly a difficult thing to recognize and acknowledge yourself as your own enemy; yet who is it really who most often stands between you and God? Who is it really who stands between you and your acceptance of Jesus Christ as Lord and Savior on a constant and regular basis? As you examine the depths of your relationship with the Holy Trinity, take a close look at those times, those situations in which you can recognize how you did in fact stand between yourself and God. Reflect how when God showed you a way to traverse across the chasm, you did not trust that way and took the route of your own choosing instead. Examine how when you did at last choose to grasp hold of God's hand how wonderful it was to know that God was in control of your life and would lead you to a place of safety.

Prayer: O God to whom I can always come in my time of need, I come to you again in this moment of need to confess before you that I and I alone have often created the chasm that often exists between you and me.   I would like to blame it on human weakness.   I would like to accuse someone other than myself.   However, if I am going to be honest with myself and with you, O Lord, then I need to confess my part in this perceived separation.   I call it a perceived separation because I am aware that you never left my side.   It was I who departed.   What joy came to me when I reached out to you, Lord, and found your Hand of Grace and Salvation already outstretched to me.   What a blessing you are in my life. Help me, Lord, to not be the enemy; not to myself nor to any other of your children.   Grant that I shall truly become that person you created me to be; and grant that I may always be found giving praise and thanksgiving to your holy name.   Amen.

*****

Tuesday of Week Four

Scripture Readings:

Psalter: Psalm 78:1-39

Old Testament: Jeremiah 7:21-34

Epistle: Romans 4:13-25

Gospel: John 7:37-52

Meditation: The Psalmist lifts his voice to the people saying, "Give ear, O my people, to my teaching; incline your ears to the words of my mouth" (Psalm 78:1)! The Psalmist is lifting up the painful history of a people who have routinely disobeyed God and equally have routinely failed to offer gratitude to the Author of their salvation. Can you not almost hear God echoing the words of the Psalmist, "Give ear to my teachings?" During this period of self-evaluation give prayerful thought to those times when you did in fact hear and understand God's teaching but made the decision to not listen to those teachings. Give thought to those times when you fall short of God's glory by choosing to not offer to God your gratitude for both the generalities and specifics of divine grace in your life. Give thought to those times when other priorities in your life took that time which truly belonged to God.

Prayer: Holy God who teaches me what it means to live as a child of God, I come to you in the midst of this Lenten season offering to you my prayer of deepest regret that I have so often failed to listen or to heed your Holy Word. I confess to you, Holy God, that I often do not take the time to thank you or to live in gratitude for all the wonderful blessings you have bestowed upon me. Truly you are God of Compassion. You show that compassion to me, a sinner, on a regular basis. I pray that you will forgive me once more for my transgressions against you. I pray that you will encourage my heart to offer thanksgiving and praise to your wonderful name. I pray that you will never leave my side; that when I am weak, your strength will prevail; when I feel downtrodden, your mercy will prevail; and when I feel so alone and lost in this world, your love and compassion shall truly prevail. Turn my heart toward you on a regular basis. This is my prayer to you. Amen

*****

Wednesday of Week Four

Scripture Readings:

Psalter: Psalm 81

Old Testament: Jeremiah 8:18-9:6

Epistle: Romans 5:1-11

Gospel: John 8:12-20

Meditation: While in the treasury Jesus was talking with some of the Pharisees. Jesus said, "I am the light of the world; he who follows me will not walk in darkness, but will have the light of life" (John 8:12). When Jesus speaks of being the light of the world, many thoughts can come to our minds. The light of the world can be that which shows the true nature of the world. In other words, the world cannot hide in darkness. Since Jesus is the light of the world, and you are in the world, then Jesus' light equally shines upon you, revealing all there is to know and be seen by God. The light of the world can also be that beacon toward which we move. In Jesus' case, He is the light of salvation. If you notice your shadow on a sunny day, you will take note that if you are walking toward the sun (the light) then your path is well lit. However, if you are walking away from the sun (the light) then you are walking in your own shadow – you are walking in darkness. During this day, meditate upon your walk in life. Have you been walking toward the light, or have you been walking away from the light? When you walked away from the light of Christ how did it make you feel?

Prayer: Blessed Light of the World, I come to you confessing that I have not always walked toward your light. I have often times walked in the darkness of my own failing to be the person you have called me to be. You set me in this world, O Lord, giving me direction and encouragement. Yet, there remain those times when I did not take that direction or your encouragement. There are those times I created my own darkness and stumbled my way through it solely because I had allowed myself to drift away from you. Forgive me, I pray, for sometimes choosing to walk in darkness. Forgive me for failing to put all of my hope, my faith and my trust in you. Remind me again and again, Lord, that you are indeed the light of this world, the light of my life, and I yearn to walk daily in your presence. Continue, I pray, to guide me to and along those pathways you would have me traverse. When I begin to drift off the path, give me a nudge back in the right direction. I ask this in the name of the one who is truly the light of my life, even Jesus Christ, my Lord and my Savior. Amen

*****

Thursday of Week Four

Scripture Readings:

Psalter: Psalm 86

Old Testament: Jeremiah 10:11-24

Epistle: Romans 5:12-21

Gospel: John 8:21-32

Meditation: When Jesus says, "When you have lifted up the Son of man" (John 8:27b). He is speaking about when He is lifted up on the cross. These words are very telling, carrying with them the heavy weight of conviction. It is too easy to think of Jesus as being lifted up on the cross by those who lived so long ago. Yet in the timeless history of the world and Christendom there are times that Jesus continues to be lifted upon the cross. There are times when the nails are again driven through His hands and feet. Today as you meditate upon Jesus' journey to the cross, reflect upon those times that you have joined with those who nailed Jesus' hands and feet and lifted him up. How horrible this thought must be. Yet the reality is that when you deny Jesus as did Peter, when you stand by and do nothing in support of the teaching and ministry of Christ as so many did, or when you simply join the crowd and follow the beat of the drum being beaten by the everyday world, truly you have lifted Jesus upon the cross. When you walk in the light of salvation, you have removed Jesus from the cross because you are living as one who is saved by Christ. But when you walk in the darkness you keep Jesus upon the cross, suffering in anguish over the weight of your sins.

Prayer: Holy God who sent His Son into the world to save the world, I thank you and praise your Holy Name that I am able to worship this day, and to know and experience the joy of forgiveness because you chose to take the act of crucifixion and turn it into a moment of glory. You allowed your Son, Jesus, to take the weight of my sins upon himself that I might be free. You allowed Jesus to die my death that I would not have to experience true death. In the midst of my own sin I was one for whom Jesus spoke when He said, "Father forgive him/her, for they know not what they are doing". Forgive me, Lord, time and time again for my weakness. Forgive me for taking Jesus' act of Salvation for granted. Forgive me for not living as a saved soul. I humbly ask and beg this of you in the Name of Jesus Christ. Amen.

*****

Friday of Week Four

Scripture Readings:

Psalter: Psalm 91

Old Testament: Jeremiah 11:1-8, 14-20

Epistle: Romans 6:1-11

Gospel: John 8:33-47

Meditation: The Psalmist meditates upon God as the True Protector of those who are faithful. He says, "He who dwells in the shelter of the Most High, who abides in the shadow of the Almighty, will say to the Lord, 'My refuge and my fortress; my God in whom I trust" (Psalm 81:1-2). We become so involved in our lives and in the continual faster paced world that we often times take the protection of God for granted. Where would we frail human beings be if it were not for the protection of God? Moreover, we need to remember that our physical wellbeing is not the totality or even the most important part of being in the shadow of the Most High. Remember that God is Spirit. Remember that you are made in the image of God; that you are also spirit. It is that spirit that grows in the strength and maturity of God. It is your spirit that needs the spiritual bread that God offers through Jesus Christ. When we dwell in the shelter of the Most High, we are living in the protective world God provides. We can, as Jesus said, be in this world, but not of this world. The world of forgiveness is no less protective than any other form of protection coming from God. Meditate this day upon the question of your faithfulness. Meditate upon the angst in your life when you even momentarily stepped outside the protective shelter of God. Mediate upon your need and your joy that God is truly your refuge.

Prayer: O Holy God who is truly my Refuge, I come to you in these moments offering to you my humble praise and gratitude in the knowledge that you love me in a way I cannot understand; yet you love me also in a way that protects me from all in this world that would assail my life; all that would draw me away from you; and all that would dig a deep chasm between us. When I think, O God, of your protection, I not only think of my physical self, but more importantly I am thinking of my spiritual self – that which is made in your image. I pray that you will continue to protect and nourish my spirit. I pray that regardless of what happens to my physical self, my spiritual self will always be true to the source of its creation, God. I acknowledge that if it were not for your protection, I would have long ago been beaten down by this world in which I find myself. You are always my help in times of trouble and thus I thank you from the depths of my heart. Amen.

*****

Saturday of Week Four

Scripture Readings:

Psalter: Psalm 90

Old Testament: Jeremiah 13:1-11

Epistle: Romans 6:12-23

Gospel: John 8:47-59

Meditation: The Word of God came to Jeremiah saying, "[Those people] who refuse to hear my words, who stubbornly follow their own heart and have gone after other gods to serve them and worship them, shall be ...... good for nothing" (Jeremiah 13:10). When we read what by some are considered to be very harsh words coming from God there is a tendency to feel and even say to oneself, "Thank goodness God isn't talking about me!" But wait; perhaps God is talking about you. Meditate this day in honesty before God. As you do, meditate upon those times when you have been really, really stubborn; times when you knew exactly what God was calling you to do, or where God was calling you to go. Did you become good for nothing when you chose to follow the dictates of your own heart and mind instead of following the will and Word of God? You may say, "But I have not gone after other gods!" Yet give thought to what it means to go to another god. It means taking the word and guidance of this other god over that of the one and only true God. In other words, when you place your will above the will of God you have made yourself a god of your own choosing; one who you will follow, at least in the moment, rather than the God of all creation, love and compassion.

Prayer: Holy God of Heaven and Earth, I come to you with a heavy heart knowing that I need to confess that there are times I have given myself god status and chose my own will and guidance rather than listening to your Word and following your guidance. I confess to you that when I (list sometimes you have made yourself god) I was truly making myself god. I began to amount to nothing. As I reflect upon these acts, O Lord, I come before you acknowledging my sinfulness; acknowledging that I felt alone and apart from you when I tried to make myself a god. Compassionate God, I pray that you will forgive me for falling so short of your will for me. I pray your forgiveness for thinking my way was somehow better than your way. I pray that you will continue to be with me, lifting me up to be the person you called, and are calling, me to be. You know me better, Lord, than I know myself. Lord, grant that I will once again live and participate in your covenant. Thank you for continuing to be present for me. Thank you for your forgiveness. Thank you for not leaving me to my own devices. I make this prayer in the name of Jesus Christ, my Lord and my Savior. Amen

*****

Sunday of Week Four

Scripture Readings:

Psalter: Psalm 66

Old Testament: Jeremiah 14:1-9, 17-22

Epistle: Galatians 4:21-5:1

Gospel: Matthew 16:1-4

Meditation: Psalm 66 is truly a Psalm of thanksgiving and praise to God. The real invitation in the words of Psalm 66 is, "Come and see what God has done" (Psalm 66:5a). Then you will know why it is that you should "Make a joyful noise to God." (Psalm 66:1a). Like so many things it sounds so easy and simple on the surface. But like so many other things in our life we tend to put off responding to that great and joyous invitation. We have all said, "Sometime we need to do such and such", or "Someday we will actually get together." We learn from experience that "sometime" and "Someday" are not on the calendar and seldom if ever come around. As you examine your current relationship with God, give thought to when was the last time you accepted the invitation to come and see what God has done in your life. When you have neglected to respond to that invitation, chances are you have equally failed to make a joyful noise to the Lord. When was the last time you made a joyful noise unto God in praise and thanksgiving for all that God has done for you? What have you done besides saying thank you? Has what God has done for you changed the way you choose to live?

Prayer: O Holy God whose very Word brings action into this world and into my life, I come to you having given great thought to all the many things you have done in my life and all the many ways you have blessed me. I especially remember when (pray about specifics of what God has done for you). You did these things, Lord, not because you had to, but because, in your love, you chose to do so. I thank you, Lord, and praise your Holy Name for all these benevolent acts. I pray that you will help me to not just utter words of gratitude. Help me also, Lord, to truly live my life in response to you, in response to your acts of love and compassion, and in response to knowing first-hand the presence and power of the Holy Spirit. I humbly ask this prayer in Jesus' name. Amen.

*****

WEEK FIVE OF LENT

Monday of Week Five

Scripture Readings:

Psalter: Psalm 89:1-18

Old Testament: Jeremiah 16:10-21

Epistle: Romans 7:1-12

Gospel: John 6:1-15

Meditation: The very familiar story of the feeding of the crowd with only a few loaves of bread and a few small fish (John 6:1-15) is one of those stories that has been told and preached upon countless times through the ages. This miracle is actually the "only" miracle that is found in all four of the gospel accounts. This alone brings the story to a certain level of importance to Christianity. While the gospel accounts vary slightly in some of the details of the miracle, the crux of the story cannot be mistaken. The power and the great message that is resident in the miracle of the loaves and fishes is this: What was not sufficient in the hands of humanity was more than sufficient in the hands of God. As you continue to examine your life with God, meditate upon those times in your life when in your hands, certain things were simply not sufficient. Yet, when you handed these situations over to God, they became more than sufficient.

Prayer: Holy God of countless miracles, I can remember easily so many times when I personally felt inadequate. Yet in your hands, I became adequate for the task at hand. I remember so many times when my energy for the day was lacking and inadequate. When I turned my day over to you, I was able to get through the day. I have seen times when available resources did not add up mathematically when compared to the bills. Yet, when I turned the situation over to you, somehow all the bills were paid and there were even a few dollars left over. I remember when on my own I did not know the right words to say. Yet, when I put the situation in your hands, you gave me the words. There are so many more times like (list some very specific times when what inadequacies you had were more than enough when given to God). So, Lord, it is now time to say thank you. It is time for me to praise you and to ask your help yet again as I strive to live a better life; as I strive to live a life that is truly in response to your love for me and for all humanity. So, once again, Lord, I place myself in your loving care. Amen.

*****

Tuesday of Week Five

Scripture Readings:

Psalter: Psalm 100

Old Testament: Jeremiah 17:19-27

Epistle: Romans 7:13-25

Gospel: John 6:16-27

Meditation: "When the disciples were in the boat about three or four miles from shore, they became frightened when they saw Jesus walking on the water toward them" (John 6:19). The disciples were naturally frightened as they witnessed Jesus walking on the water. Three to four miles from shore is not exactly where the disciples would have expected to find Jesus. One of the great lessons to learn from this story is to not be at all surprised where in your life you find Jesus showing up. You may think there are parts of your life where Jesus could never be. Yet, the story of Jesus walking on water four miles out to sea should help you to realize there are no places in your life where you will not find Jesus. There are times you will no doubt hope Jesus does not show up because you would be really embarrassed to have Him find you in the situation you are in, or to find you doing what you are doing. Meditate today upon some times when you have found yourself in a dark place, and yet the light of Christ came to you. Meditate upon some times when you were frightened until you could sense the voice of Jesus saying, "It is I; do not be afraid." (John 6:20b).

Prayer: O Holy God who in Jesus Christ chose to walk atop the waters of the sea to bring the message that we should not be afraid, I come to you in these moments to remember and acknowledge those times when you showed up in some very dark places in my life. I admit, Lord, there have been a few times I actually gave up, wondering if you were really active in my life. There were times when I was angry with you because I felt you let me down. There were times I have felt you did not answer my prayer. Precious Lord, I pray your forgiveness for not placing more hope and trust in you. I pray that you will forgive me for not being happy with your time frame. I pray that you will forgive me for getting angry and wondering where you were. I was so blinded by the immensity of my problem I failed to see at first your glorious presence. Little by little, Lord, I am coming around. With your help I will be able to move through life once more with a sense of hope and joy. With your help I will be able to live as one who knows the power of God, and one who knows first-hand the love of God. Bless me, Lord, as I continue to trust you with my life. Amen

*****

Wednesday of Week Five

Scripture Readings:

Psalter: Psalm 101

Old Testament: Jeremiah 18:1-11

Epistle: Romans 8:1-11

Gospel: John 6:27-40

Meditation: David, the Psalmist, said, "I will sing of loyalty and of justice; to Thee, O Lord, I will sing" (Psalm 101:1). The loyalty David is talking about in the Psalm is of a king who will rule justly. There are those who speculate that he is talking about himself. The king is singing to God that he will be loyal to those over whom he is to be kind. He will be kind and just. By being a child of God, and by being a disciple of Jesus Christ, you are one who is in charge of teaching others. So, the question of justice and loyalty come for you in the life you choose to live. As a child of God you are setting an example in the world and in the community in which you live. Are you loyal to God and to Jesus Christ in the living of your life and in the example you are setting for those around you? Do you offer justice to those in your life who have caused pain to you or to another? Certainly, as King of Kings, God in Jesus Christ is loyal to you. But where do you stand? If your life were to be the test for what it means to be loyal to God, to Jesus, to the Holy Spirit, and to the life you know you have been called to live, what kind of example are you presenting? Have you sung promises of loyalty to God? Have you followed God's example of justice?

Prayer: O Holy God who is truly King of Kings, there are times in my life when I know I have not rendered justice unto others in the same portion I would wish it to be rendered unto me. I have eagerly accepted your justice for me, but have been slow in passing on that same justice to others. I find it difficult sometimes to do the right thing. I get in my own way. I pray, Lord, that you will forgive me for times when I could have rendered more justice than I did. I remember especially the time (list a time when you could have done a better job at rendering justice). Lord, in these moments I pledge my loyalty to you. In doing so I am confident that I will learn to live with a greater sense of loyalty and justice. I realize that if I pledge my loyalty first to you, then it will be much easier to pledge my loyalty and my justice to those in my life. Thank you, Holy God, for the wonderful gift of loyalty. Amen.

*****

Thursday of Week Five

Scripture Readings:

Psalter: Psalm 69

Old Testament: Jeremiah 22:13-23

Epistle: Romans 8:12-27

Gospel: John 6:41-51

Meditation: Jesus said, "I am the living bread which came down from heaven; if any one eats of this bread, he will live forever" (John 6:54). So often we spend too much of our time thinking about the things of this world. It is that which we can hold, touch, see, examine which most often grabs and keeps our attention. Today we spend much of our attention on food for the physical body. We are very anxious to make sure we eat only the right food and only the right amount of food. We are sure this, along with proper exercise, is the only way to get our physical body in shape. Yet, we soon forget that our physical body is nothing but a vessel of clay which contains our spiritual body. It is our spiritual body that is made in God's image. It is our spiritual body that will be born to eternal life. It is sad but true that most people put far more emphasis on taking care of the physical body than they do the spiritual body. Where is your attention? Where to you place the emphasis? Do you yearn for the spiritual food that only God can provide? Do you seek to get your spiritual body in shape and keep it that way?

Prayer: God of Spirit who created me in His own divine image, I pray your forgiveness for those times when I have not lived as one created in the image of God. I pray your forgiveness for those times I worried more about the condition of my physical body than the condition of my spiritual body. Feed me, Lord, I pray. Feed me that spiritual food that will nourish my spiritual body. Help me to exercise my spiritual muscles such that I will truly be living in this world as one who is made in your image. I make this prayer in Jesus' Name. Amen.

*****

Friday of Week Five

Scripture Readings:

Psalter: Psalm 107:1-32

Old Testament: Jeremiah 23:1-8

Epistle: Romans 8:28-39

Gospel: John 6:52-59

Meditation: The Word of God came to Jeremiah saying "Woe to the shepherds who destroy and scatter the sheep of my pasture" (Jeremiah 23:1)! The natural question at this point is to inquire how can we as everyday people destroy and scatter the sheep of God's pasture. The simple answer is that when we offer a bad example of what it means to be Christian; when we offer a bad example of what it means to be child of God, then we have destroyed the sheep of God's pasture because we have steered them away from God and away from what it truly means to be Christian. It is not only our actions of commission, but also our acts of omission that cause us to scatter God's sheep. Reflect upon when you have offered a bad example of what it means to be a Christian. Reflect upon a time when you steered one of God's sheep in another direction.

Prayer: God of Love and Mercy, I come to you at this time to ask your forgiveness for every time I have alone, or in conjunction with others, scattered your sheep. I seek your forgiveness for those times when I have destroyed the relationship that you have worked so hard to build. Holy God, enter my heart once more. As you heal me of my affliction, I pray you will also open my heart, mind, and very soul to the example I need to be setting as a child of God.   Bless me, Lord, as I become more and more like that person you knew I could be when, before I was even born, you called me by name. Even as Jesus Christ is the Good Shepherd, I pray that I, also, will be a good shepherd for the sheep of your pasture. Amen.

*****

Saturday of Week Five

Scripture Readings:

Psalter: Psalm 108

Old Testament: Jeremiah 23:9-15

Epistle: Romans 9:1-18

Gospel: John 6:60-71

Meditation: "After this many of [Jesus'] disciples drew back and no longer went about with him. Jesus said to the twelve, 'Do you also wish to go away (John 6:66-67)?'" We can only imagine what the twelve original disciples must have been thinking when Jesus asked them if they also wished to go away. Some of Jesus' teachings were hard to hear. Jesus was laying it out as clearly as He possibly could that being His disciple is not an easy task. Today as you meditate upon these readings, think about what it means to be a Christian. Do you at times find that being a Christian is too difficult? Do you find yourself sometimes wanting to pick the parts you like and disregard the rest? What would be your reaction if Jesus asked you, "Do you also wish to go away?"

Prayer: Holy God, forbid that I should ever seek to go away. I confess to you, Lord, that I do sometimes find it to be very difficult to be a Christian in a world that can at times be overwhelmingly hostile. I have at times wished I could just choose those things about Christianity that I like, but ignore the things I do not like. For these things I can only ask you to forgive me. You know better than I, Lord that I find it difficult to adhere to some of Jesus' teachings, especially (list a teaching that you find difficult to follow). I pray, Holy God that you will guide me and protect me such that I can truly be the Christian I know you call me to be. Help me to learn to trust and obey the teachings of Jesus. It is in His Holy Name that I make this prayer. Amen.

*****

Sunday of Week Five

Scripture Readings:

Psalter: Psalm 145

Old Testament: Jeremiah 23:16-32

Epistle: 1 Corinthians 9:19-27

Gospel: Matthew 16:24-28

Meditation: "Then Jesus told His disciples, 'If any man would come after me, let him deny himself and take up his cross and follow me'" (Matthew 16:24). To deny ourselves is quite the undertaking. It means to truly turn our attention away from our own worldly desires and focus on Christ within. The Apostle Paul said it quite well in his letter to the Church at Galatia when he wrote, "It is no longer I who live, but Christ who lives in me." (Galatians 2:20). So then Jesus asks us to deny ourselves, but also to take up our cross and follow Him. The key to Jesus' words is that we are to pick up "our" cross, not His cross, and not someone else's cross. We need only be concerned with our cross. We can interpret the carrying of our cross in many ways. For the purposes of this meditation let's think of it as carrying our own baggage; carrying our own sense of unworthiness; carrying the weight of our sin because we have not fully given it over to Christ. As you meditate today, give deep thought to whether or not you actually deny yourself. Perhaps you only partially deny yourself. Do you allow your own self to occupy that space within where Christ seeks to live? Do you pick up your cross and follow Jesus?

Prayer: God of all who seek to follow Christ, I come to you in these quiet moments confessing to you that I do not always deny myself as I should. This world in which I live has become such a "me" world that I often have difficulty being in the world but not of the world. I confess to you, Lord that I could do a better job of allowing Christ within me to come forth. I also confess that I could do a better job of picking up my cross, my sins, my baggage and following you. Bless me, Lord, and help me with this endeavor to truly be a disciple of Christ and a child of God. Help me to follow Jesus Christ such that in losing my life, I shall truly find it. I ask this in the name of the one who gave himself as ransom for me, even Jesus Christ, my Lord and my Savior. Amen.

*****

WEEK SIX OF LENT

Monday of Week Six

Scripture Readings:

Psalter: Psalm 35

Old Testament: Jeremiah 24:1-10

Epistle: Romans 9:19-33

Gospel: John 9:1-17

Meditation: Jesus said, "As long as I am in the world, I am the light of the world." (John 9:5). He spoke these words after healing a man who had been blind since birth. It is interesting that Jesus refers to himself as the light of the world after helping a man bring light into his own life for the first time since birth. As long as Christians continue to have Jesus in their hearts, He will continue to be in this world. While it would be good to say that we are now the light of the world, the truth is that Jesus continues to be the light of the world as long as we let Him shine brightly in the life we live. As you meditate today, give thought to the question of to what extent you allow the light of Christ to shine through you. Are you prone to hide it under a bushel? Or are you more prone to lift it high as an example for all to see?

Prayer: Holy God who in Jesus Christ holds himself out to be the light of the world, I confess that I have not always allowed or encouraged the light of Christ to shine through my life. For this I am truly sorry. I have not always led a life that would demonstrate the light of Christ to those around me. For this I am also truly sorry. I confess that all too often I allow my own dim light to come forth. Precious Lord, I pray that you will have mercy upon me, a sinner, and forgive me for these and all my transgressions against you. Give me guidance each moment of every day that I may live in a way that encourages the light of Christ to shine forth in the life I live. Grant that I will do my part to help to make this world a better place in which to live by spreading the light of Christ wherever I go. I ask this in the name of one who is truly the light of the world, even Jesus Christ, my Lord and my Savior. Amen.

*****

Tuesday of Week Six

Scripture Readings:

Psalter: Psalm 121

Old Testament: Jeremiah 25:8-17

Epistle: Romans 10:1-13

Gospel: John 9:18-41

Meditation: The continuing story of the man blind since birth that Jesus healed brings us to the point of discussing the true power of God. One may ask why Jesus would heal a blind man and yet leave so many others with physical ailments unchanged. The primary reason is that God did not send Jesus into the world to bring about physical healings. "God sent Jesus into the world, not to condemn the world, but that the world might be saved through him" (John 3:17). So, it is for our salvation that Jesus came into the world and daily comes into our lives. It is not for the healing of our physical bodies. When God through Jesus Christ heals physical bodies it is a way of showing the true power of God. It is the full depth and breadth of a miracle. The question for you to meditate upon today is this: Do you choose to spend your time and energy seeking physical healing which at best will only be temporary, or do you choose to spend your time and your energy seeking spiritual healing which shall inherit eternal life?

Prayer: Holy God who can bring change to the world, as I look honestly at myself this day I confess that I do spend a great deal of time concerned with my physical health. It is easy to say it is human nature to do so. Yet, I know that you call me to accept the saving acts of Jesus Christ, not to spend my time dwelling on the physical. Sometimes the physical body can be in pain. It is in the midst of this suffering that I pray for relief. Help me, Lord, to focus my attention upon the saving acts of Jesus Christ. Help me to give you all praise and all glory for truly you are the Author of my salvation. I thank you with all my heart, through Jesus Christ, my Savior. Amen.

*****

Wednesday of Week Six

Scripture Readings:

Psalter: Psalm 130

Old Testament: Jeremiah 25:30-38

Epistle: Romans 10:14-21

Gospel: John 10:1-18

Meditation: Jesus says, "I am the Good Shepherd. The Good Shepherd lays down his life for the sheep." (John 10:11). Jesus also says, "The hireling flees because he is a hireling and cares nothing for the sheep." (John 10:13). Jesus holds Himself out as the example of the Good Shepherd who lays down His life for the sheep, those over whom God has asked Him to watch and protect. Jesus then contrasts the attitude of the Good Shepherd with that of the hireling who cares nothing for the sheep. In reviewing this obvious contrast we are taught the very important lesson that as Christians we are called to be shepherds of sheep, shepherds of one another. The question being raised is will we indeed serve in the capacity of shepherd, laying down our own life for others; or will we in the final analysis serve as one who is a hireling, ultimately running away when the situation is too tough for us to handle? Laying down our life does not mean being nailed to a cross. Rather, laying down our life means to focus on the needs of the other person, and not so much on our own needs. It means to make sacrifices, if and when necessary, to make sure that fellow humans are cared for. As you meditate upon the scriptures for today, give thought to whether your life is one of being a shepherd or whether it is one of being a hireling. In talking with God, can you point to concrete examples?

Prayer: Holy and Gracious God who in Jesus Christ is indeed the Good Shepherd, I come to you in this time set aside for prayer that I might offer to you my deepest gratitude for caring for me and all of humanity. I thank you for calling me to also be a good shepherd in those places you lead me, and for those people and situations to whom you lead me. I pray, Lord, for forgiveness for those times in which I behaved more like a hireling than a shepherd. I pray that you will forgive me for abandoning others of your sheep in their time of need. Grant Holy God that I will strive to be the best shepherd I can be. Grant that never again will I take on the role of a hireling. Encourage me to use Jesus, the Good Shepherd, as my constant example. It is in His Holy Name that I ask this prayer. Amen

*****

Thursday of Week Six

Scripture Readings:

Psalter: Psalm 140

Old Testament: Jeremiah 26:1-16

Epistle: Romans 11:1-12

Gospel: John 10:19-42

Meditation: "So the Jews gathered round [Jesus] and said to him, 'How long will you keep us in suspense? If you are the Christ, tell us plainly'" (John 10:24). Jesus points to his works and says they bear witness to who he is. In other words, Jesus wants the Jews to decide for themselves whether or not He is the Christ of God rather than saying so himself. The question for you to ponder today is whether or not, with your whole being, you proclaim Jesus to be the Christ of God. Do you sometimes wonder if you believe what you believe because you believe it; or if you believe what you believe because you were taught to believe it? For you, is Jesus the Son of God? For you, is Jesus the Messiah promised by God? For you, is the crucified and risen Christ the source of your salvation? If you answer this question in the affirmative, is it because of what you think; because of what you hope; because of your experience in life; or because of your faith?

Prayer: Holy God and Father of Jesus Christ, I come to you today first of all just to be close to you. In your presence I can feel truly alive. I can sense both the gentleness and the power of your presence. Lord, I know that I have proclaimed Jesus as the Christ. I have equally proclaimed Jesus as my Lord and Savior. Sometimes my proclamation is hampered by periods of confusion, periods of doubt, and periods of wondering if I have made the right decision. But after sitting with you for a while, Lord, I can with confidence continue to go forth in the world proclaiming Jesus Christ as Messiah, as Lord and Savior. I pray that you will forgive me for those times when questioning and doubt slipped in. I pray that you will help me to not waver from my conviction that you have granted me the gift of salvation through the saving acts of Jesus Christ. I ask this in the name of Jesus. Amen.

*****

Friday of Week Six

Scripture Readings:

Psalter: Psalm 143

Old Testament: Jeremiah 29:1, 4-13

Epistle: Romans 11:13-24

Gospel: Matthew 18:1-6

Meditation: When the disciples began to ask Jesus about the kingdom of heaven, they asked who would be the greatest. "And calling to him a child, [Jesus] put him in the midst of them, and said, 'Truly, I say to you, unless you turn and become like children, you will never enter the kingdom of heaven'" (Matthew 18:2). With these words Jesus is talking about faith. The children accept everything on faith. The adults all too often try to analyze everything beyond recognition. Indeed adults tend to complicate the simplicity of faith. As we get closer to the beginning of Holy Week, take time today to meditate upon your level of faith. When you go to the doctor or to the hospital and they ask about your pain level, generally they are asking on a scale of 1 to 10 where is your pain. So, on a scale of 1 to 10, with 10 being the highest score possible, where is your level of faith? Do you believe unconditionally? Do you believe up to a point? Do you believe such that you have in every way accepted Jesus Christ as your Lord and Savior?

Prayer: O Holy God who has blessed me in more ways than I can count, I confess that I do not ponder who will be the greatest in heaven. However, I do often concern myself with whether or not a person's level of faith makes a difference. I confess that sometimes my faith has wavered. This is especially true when I have prayed long and earnestly and yet my prayers seem to fall upon deaf ears. I confess that sometimes I make faith too complicated by trying to examine every detail. I recognize that this weakness in faith is attributed to my own moments of doubt. Grant me, Lord, to have the faith and trust of a child. Grant that I might respond to your love in such a way as to be pleasing in your sight. Grant that I might truly live, praising you and giving you all glory, even as my faith becomes more and more like that of a child. I ask this in Jesus' Holy Name. Amen.

*****

Saturday of Week Six

Scripture Readings:

Psalter: Psalm 43

Old Testament: Jeremiah 31:27-34

Epistle: Romans 11:25-36

Gospel: John 11:28-44

Meditation: The Psalmist inquires of himself, "Why are you cast down, O my soul, and why are you disquieted within me? Hope in God; for I shall again praise him, my help and my God" (Psalm 43:5). Have you ever felt that your very soul was disquieted? Have you felt cast down? These are very powerful questions based on strong language used by the Psalmist. To be disquieted means to have a total lack of calm, or ease, or peace. It is to be anxious, uneasy or discomposed. To be cast down is to feel discouraged or dejected. The Psalmist is saying ever so eloquently that if you do in fact become disquieted or if you ever feel cast down, then take refuge in God. He encourages you to put your hope in God, knowing that you will once again praise God. Today you are encouraged to meditate and reflect upon your own sense of being disquieted, or your own sense of feeling cast down. Do you feel this way because of the way of the world? Do you perhaps feel this way toward God?

Prayer: Holy God, I come to you to confess that there are indeed those times when my very soul feels disquieted. There are those times when my soul feels cast down. Sometimes it is because of circumstances in my own life over which I apparently have no control. Sometimes it is because my world seems to fall in around me and I am burdened by the weight of its heavy pieces. Sometimes it is because I have turned away from you in my anguish. Forgive me I pray. Lift me up, O Lord, and encourage me to return to you. Grant that I will once more place my hope in you. You are truly the God of my refuge. In you I can be open and honest. In you I can feel comforted. In you I will know once again that great peace that can come only from you. Bless me, Lord, as I come to you, ever singing your praises. Amen.

*****

Palm Sunday

Scripture Readings:

Psalter: Psalm 118:1-2, 19-29

Gospel: Matthew 21:1-11

Meditation: In Matthew's account of the Gospel, he tells us that "most of the crowd spread their garments on the road and others cut branches from the trees and spread them on the road" as Jesus rode by on a donkey (Matthew 21:8). This custom in Jesus' day was meant to be an honor. It shows the true feelings of those who stand along the way. When it comes to your relationship with Jesus, He is not looking to be honored by the laying of your coat or by the spreading of branches. Jesus is looking to be honored by the way you live. So the question for you to ponder today is how do you honor Jesus? Do you honor Jesus with the way you live your life? Where have you fallen short? What can you do to live a life which will honor Jesus all the more?

Prayer: O Holy God, you are truly worthy of more praise than I could possibly give. I have come to understand that you do not look for sacrifices brought to the altar. Rather you look for lives that are lived in response to your love and to the saving acts of Jesus Christ. Holy God, bless me as I strive to do just that. Bless me as I strive to honor God who brought me into being; and bless me as I strive to honor Jesus Christ by living as close to His example as possible. Help me, Lord, to not concern myself with the laying down of branches or coats, but rather may I concern myself with the laying down of my life in grateful response to the love, grace and mercy of God the Father, God the Son, and God the Holy Spirit. Amen.

*****

HOLY WEEK

Monday of Holy Week

Scripture Readings:

Psalter: Psalm 36:5-11

Old Testament: Isaiah 42:1-9

Epistle: Hebrews 9:11-15

Gospel: John 12:1-11

Meditation: The familiar story of Mary and Martha serving Jesus in their own way is a story that is forever relevant (John 12:1-8). The basis of the story is that Jesus is saying there are multiple ways of serving. We need to find that way of serving, not that we like best, but that through discernment we are confident God is calling us to. Today is a day to reflect upon how it is that you serve God, Christ, the Holy Spirit, and the Church. Do you serve the way you prefer to serve even if God is calling you in a different direction? Is your way of serving what is best for you or is it what is best for the Church and/or the community?

Prayer: Holy God who bestows gifts upon me through the Holy Spirit, I pray this day that you will help me to discern if I am truly serving in the way you have called me to serve, or if I am serving in the way I like best. Forgive me, Lord, when I have been so busy doing things my way that I have been unable to hear or recognize your call to me to move in a new and different direction. Grant that I will with earnest endeavor to understand the way you want me to serve in any given situation. I acknowledge that service can change from need to need. I acknowledge that as I traverse through this earthly life I will find multiple ways to serve, and for this glorious gift I give you my thanks and my praise. Amen.

*****

Tuesday of Holy Week

Scripture Readings:

Psalter: Psalm 71:1-14

Old Testament: Isaiah 49:1-7

Epistle: 1 Corinthians 1:18-31

Gospel: John 12:20-36

Meditation: Jesus was at the point, not only of knowing the pain and suffering that was to come, but He also began to talk about it more openly. In our Christian faith we talk of Jesus being wholly human and wholly divine. It is the two natures of Christ represented by the two candles on the altar table. The human part of Jesus exclaimed, "Now is my soul troubled. And what shall I say? 'Father, save me from this hour'? No, for this purpose I have come to this hour" (John12:27). This is a very important piece of Scripture. It points out that Jesus knows first-hand the pain of anguish. It points out that a little piece of Him would like to change the course of events. Yet, in the final analysis, Jesus knows why God has put Him on this earth. Jesus knows what God has asked Him to do. Jesus knows, no matter how difficult and unpleasant the task may be He has chosen to do the will of God. Today as you reflect upon Scripture and look earnestly at your own life, discern those times when you really did not want to do what you knew God was asking you to do. Meditate upon the struggle with yourself over doing God's will or taking an easier path.

Prayer: Blessed Jesus who knows the depths of anguish, I thank you and praise your Holy Name for setting the example for me to follow. I thank you for accomplishing the will of God even though you knew it would be a difficult task. You know first-hand the anguish of my own soul when I recognize God calling me to do something that is truly outside my comfort zone. Your own suffering makes it easier for me to talk with you about my suffering. Your initial question of whether or not to seek a different path helps me to know that you understand my hesitation at some of God's encouragements. Holy God, forgive me, I pray for those times when I have been reluctant to follow your will because I thought the task to be too difficult for me, or I thought it to be too far outside my comfort zone. Thank you that your Son, Jesus, did set the example for me to follow. Help me always, Lord, to have the strength and courage to follow your direction. I make this prayer in the name of Jesus Christ, your Son, my Savior. Amen.

*****

Wednesday of Holy Week

Scripture Readings:

Psalter: Psalm 70

Old Testament: Isaiah 50:4-9a

Epistle: Hebrews 12:1-3

Gospel: John 13:21-32

Meditation: As Jesus sat with His disciples He said, "Truly, truly, I say to you, one of you will betray me." (John 13:21b). Of course we all know that Jesus was talking about Judas Iscariot. Yet, Jesus' words are very haunting for us today. Imagine Jesus calling you by name saying, "(your name), truly, truly, I say to you, you have betrayed me." Today is a day to give very careful thought in the depths of your soul about those times that you know Jesus was right; those times when you did betray him either by action or inaction. What caused you to betray Jesus? How did you feel afterward? Did you try to make amends?

Prayer: God of Compassion, I come to you in the quiet of these moments with a heavy heart. My heart is truly heavy as I confess to you that I have indeed betrayed Jesus. There was the time I (say how you betrayed Jesus), and then there was the time I (say another time you betrayed Jesus). Lord, there is really no excuse. I could say I was weak at the moment. I could say that Satan made me do it. But ultimately I have free will as a gift entrusted to me by you. In the exercise of my free will I made a bad decision. Indeed I made the wrong decision. I pray that you will forgive me for this and all my sins. Help me, Lord, to not betray Jesus. I know I will be tempted again. I need your help, Lord. I need your strength. I cannot do this alone. Bless me and keep me I pray. Amen.

*****

Maundy Thursday

Scripture Readings:

Psalter: Psalm 116:1-2, 12-19

Old Testament: Exodus 12:1-14

Epistle: 1 Corinthians 11:23-26

Gospel: John 13:1-17, 31b-35

Meditation: Jesus said to His disciples, "A new commandment I give to you, that you love one another; even as I have loved you, that you also love one another. By this all [people] will know that you are my disciples, if you have love for one another" (John 13:34-35). We are all so very familiar with Jesus' words, and yet it seems that we often either forget them; choose to ignore them, or simply to do not understand them. It is easy for us to speak of love for one another. But all too often these words roll too easily off our lips and are not supported by our actions, and often not supported by the true feelings of our soul. To take Jesus' words at the very depth of their meaning is to understand that Jesus is commanding us, not simply to love, but to love one another with the same depth of love that He loves us. For some, that is a tall order. Yet, it is what Jesus did, and it is what Jesus asks us to do. Today as you meditate, give thought to whether or not you love others with the same love that Jesus loves you. If your answer is no, or not always, or only sometimes, then what can you do to change that?

Prayer: Gracious and Holy God, your Son has commanded me to love others even as He loves me. I confess that I have not always loved with that same depth of love. I am not even sure I have set it as a goal I wish to achieve. Forgive me, Lord, for not following the example set by Jesus. Remind me that Jesus' words are not a suggestion; they are a command. Remind me that Jesus said it is only when I love as He has loved that people will know I am His disciple. Help me, Lord, to set as a new goal that I will strive with earnest to love others even as Jesus loves me. This will sometimes be difficult for me so I also pray that you will give me the help I need to achieve this goal. I ask this prayer in the Name of Him who set the example, Jesus Christ, your Son, my Lord Savior. Amen.

*****

Good Friday

Scripture Readings:

Psalter: Psalm 22

Old Testament: Isaiah 52:13-53:12

Epistle: Hebrews 10:16-25

Gospel: John 18:1-19:42

Meditation: In Matthew's account of the Gospel Jesus tells Peter, ""truly, I say to you, this very night, before the cock crows, you will deny me three times." (Matthew 26:34). In today's reading from John's account of the Gospel, this very prediction takes place. Peter had vowed eternal loyalty to Jesus even when others would deny Him. Jesus, however, knew that circumstances would change Peter's resolve. As you meditate upon your journey with Jesus today, take a hard and honest look within and determine when and under what circumstance you did in fact deny Jesus. It is not a matter of uttering words of disclaimer as did Peter. It is more a matter of not allowing the Christ within to guide your actions in a particular situation.

Prayer: Eternal God of all that is Holy, I come to you confessing that like Peter, if someone were to say that I would deny Jesus three times in a certain period, I would most certainly tell them I would not. It would be very difficult for me to describe myself as one who denies Jesus. Yet, Lord,

I acknowledge that when I choose to not do or say the right thing; when I choose to stand as a blockade between Jesus and another; or when I stand by and do nothing in Jesus' name then I am truly denying Jesus. In His humanity Jesus cried out from the cross, "My God, my God, why hast thou forsaken me?" (Psalm 22:1a). There are times when deep in my soul I know that Jesus must be saying, "(your name), why have you forsaken me?" I don't have a good answer, Lord. I pray for your forgiveness. I pray that you will guide me in ways that will lead me to never deny Jesus again. I humbly ask in Christ's Holy Name. Amen.

*****

Holy Saturday

Scripture Readings:

Psalter: Psalm 31:1-4, 15-16

Old Testament: Job 14:1-14

Epistle: 1 Peter 4:1-8

Gospel: John 18:1-19:42

Meditation: The reading for today from John's account of the Gospel talks simply about the laying of Jesus' body in the tomb. What is not given in this portion of the story but is certainly present in the understanding of the story, is the heavy weight of shock, disbelief, and even questionable faith that suddenly exists. Jesus was to be their leader. Jesus was sent by God. Jesus still had work to do. But the crucifixion and the resultant body lying in the tomb were all too real. What went wrong? What do we do next? As you meditate today upon the story of Jesus being placed in the tomb, give thought to the times when things did not go exactly as you had planned even though you had shared all your concerns with God. Were you not in disbelief when things did not turn out the way you expected? Being honest with yourself, didn't your faith crumble even if only for a short while? Did you not inquire from your soul why things did not turn out the way you expected?

Prayer: Merciful God, it is with great difficulty that I come before you today to confess that there have been times when I was in great shock and disbelief when things did not go as I expected. For this I humbly pray for your forgiveness. Help me to understand that even though I do not always see the larger picture the same way as you, that you do have a plan, that you are always in control, and when things work out in accordance with your will, then all is good and perfect. I confess also, Lord that in such times my faith wavers. I pray that when this happens that you will embrace me; lift me up; and remind me of the portion of Scripture that says, "But they who wait for the Lord shall renew their strength, they shall mount up with wings like eagles, they shall run and not be weary, they shall walk and not faint." (Isaiah 40:31). All of this I pray in Jesus' Holy Name. Amen

*****

Easter Sunday

Scripture Readings:

Psalter: Psalm 118:1-2, 14-24

Old Testament: Jeremiah 31:1-6

Epistle: Acts 10:34-43

Gospel: Matthew 28:1-10

Meditation: Referring to Jesus the angel said to Mary Magdalene and the other Mary, "Do not be afraid; for I know that you seek Jesus who was crucified. He is not here; for he has risen" (Matthew 28:5b-6a). Today is the day that you are invited to meditate upon what it means to you that Jesus Christ is Risen. How is your life influenced or shaped by the Resurrection? How often do you give thanks, and how do you give thanks, for the saving acts of Jesus Christ? Today is the day to give deep thought to whether you simply say the words and sing the hymns about Resurrection, or do you truly believe in Resurrection and its saving power. Christ is Risen! He is Risen Indeed!

Prayer: Holy God of the Resurrection, the human heart and mind do not contain the words that could adequately proclaim my joy in the full understanding, acknowledgement, and faith in the Resurrection of Jesus Christ. You, O Lord, took a travesty of humanity and turned it into something good and eternal. Only God could take capital punishment and turn it into an act of salvation for all humanity. Look into my soul, Lord, and know the love and gratitude that reside there, not only for the gift of salvation, but for every blessing you bestow upon humanity, upon me as an individual person, and upon those whom I love and care for. The Resurrection is truly an act of forgiveness, and yet it is also a constant reminder of the love and power of God. Bless me this day, O Lord, and help me to live the life you have given me as one who truly believes with all my heart, soul, and being that Christ is risen indeed. Amen.

*****

Epilogue

I pray that having used "In God's Grace" as a daily meditation you have known the true blessings and presence of God. I pray that you have a better understanding of yourself as a human soul created in the image of God; and that you have come to more fully understand the reality and magnitude of the saving acts of Jesus Christ. This book is not one to be taken lightly, but with an earnest aim toward self-evaluation and ultimately self-improvement as a child of God. Its purpose and direction are intended to live with you long after you have tucked it away on a shelf somewhere. If you have found this small book helpful I encourage you to let others know. It is a tool that is meant to be shared. If you have truly been blessed by your experience with this writing I encourage you to discuss the matter with those you love. When you realize fully the extent to which you are living in God's grace, it is not a revelation to be kept secret. Rather, it is a portion of the good and wonderful news that is meant to be shared with anyone who is receptive to its message.

Whether you save this book to be read and used again during the next Lenten season, or whether you use it occasionally all during the year, I pray that you will continually be personally aware that you are truly living "In God's Grace".

David H. Lester

About the Author

The Rev. Dr. David H. Lester, a minister in the Congregational tradition, received both his Master's of Divinity and Doctor of Ministry Degrees from Bangor Theological Seminary. He has spent a life time both formally and informally bringing Christ's message of hope to the marginalized. Dr. Lester is well known throughout Northern New England for his work and ministry with the spiritually poor and has published an introductory article on "Ministry with the Poor in Spirit". Among his writings as a local church historian are "Faith, Promise, and Mission: Working with a Local Congregation in the Discovery and Proclamation of its Identity" as well as a recent work "A History of East Orrington Congregational Church". Dr. Lester has written and published articles on "Access to the Eucharist" and "The Black Shirt Gang", a treatise on why he chooses to wear the clerical collar. His current work, "In God's Grace," is a reflection of his own faith journey and has already been well received by many in the Christian community. Dr. Lester currently lives in Orrington, Maine with his wife, Joyce. He is on the pastoral staff at East Orrington Congregational Church and serves as Church Historian. He serves on the Executive Committee for the Congregational Christian Council of Maine, and is a Mentoring Pastor for the Mentoring Practice Program at Bangor Theological Seminary.

*****